First World War
and Army of Occupation
War Diary
France, Belgium and Germany

3 DIVISION
7 Infantry Brigade
Worcestershire Regiment
3rd Battalion
4 August 1914 - 31 October 1915

WO95/1415/3

The Naval & Military Press Ltd
www.nmarchive.com
Published in association with The National Archives

Published by

The Naval & Military Press Ltd

Unit 10 Ridgewood Industrial Park,

Uckfield, East Sussex,

TN22 5QE England

Tel: +44 (0) 1825 749494

www.naval-military-press.com

www.nmarchive.com

This diary has been reprinted in facsimile from the original. Any imperfections are inevitably reproduced and the quality may fall short of modern type and cartographic standards.

© **Crown Copyright**
Images reproduced by permission of The National Archives, London, England, 2015.

Contents

Document type	Place/Title	Date From	Date To
Heading	WO95/1415 3 Div 7 Infantry Bde 3 Battn Worcestershire Regt Aug 1914 Oct 1915		
Heading	3rd Division 7th Infy Bde 3rd Battalion The Worcestershire Regt. Aug-Dec 1914		
Heading	7th Brigade 3rd Division 1 3rd Battalion The Worcestershire Regiment August 1914		
Heading	War Diary 3rd Bn. Worcestershire Regt. 7th Brigade Volume I 4-31.8.14		
War Diary	Tidworth	04/08/1914	14/08/1914
War Diary	Southampton	14/08/1914	14/08/1914
War Diary	Havre	15/08/1914	16/08/1914
War Diary	Aumoye	17/08/1914	17/08/1914
War Diary	Marbaix	18/08/1914	19/08/1914
War Diary	Dompierre	20/08/1914	20/08/1914
War Diary	Feignies	21/08/1914	31/08/1914
Heading	7th Brigade 3rd Division 3rd Battalion Worcestershire Regiment September 1914		
Heading	3rd Worcestershire Regt. 7th Brigade Volume II 1-30.9.14		
War Diary	Coyolles	01/09/1914	02/09/1914
War Diary	S'Souplets	03/09/1914	03/09/1914
War Diary	Sancy	04/09/1914	04/09/1914
War Diary	Les Chapelles Bourbons	05/09/1914	05/09/1914
War Diary	Farmoutiers	07/09/1914	07/09/1914
War Diary	Les Petits Avlnois	08/09/1914	08/09/1914
War Diary	Bussieres	09/09/1914	09/09/1914
War Diary	Montemafroy	10/09/1914	11/09/1914
War Diary	Cerseuil	12/09/1914	12/09/1914
War Diary	Braine	13/09/1914	13/09/1914
War Diary	Vailly	14/09/1914	15/09/1914
War Diary	Trenches Vailly	16/09/1914	21/09/1914
War Diary	Chassemy	22/09/1914	24/09/1914
War Diary	Augy	25/09/1914	30/09/1914
War Diary	7th Brigade 3rd Division 3rd Battalion Worcestershire Regiment October 1914		
Heading	3rd Worcestershire Rgt. 7th Brigade. Vol III 1-31.10.14		
War Diary	Augy	01/10/1914	01/10/1914
War Diary	Chassemy	02/10/1914	02/10/1914
War Diary	Grand Rozoy	03/10/1914	03/10/1914
War Diary	Coyolles	05/10/1914	05/10/1914
War Diary	Saintimes	06/10/1914	06/10/1914
War Diary	Picquigny	07/10/1914	07/10/1914
War Diary	Le Plessier	08/10/1914	09/10/1914
War Diary	Pernes	10/10/1914	11/10/1914
War Diary	Lannoy	12/10/1914	12/10/1914
War Diary	Near Lacoutre	13/10/1914	13/10/1914
War Diary	Richebourg St Vaast	14/10/1914	16/10/1914
War Diary	Bois De Biez	17/10/1914	17/10/1914
War Diary	Le Hue	18/10/1914	18/10/1914
War Diary	Bois De Biez	19/10/1914	20/10/1914

War Diary	Le Hue		21/10/1914	22/10/1914
War Diary	Rue Du Marais		23/10/1914	23/10/1914
War Diary	La Quinque Rue		24/10/1914	30/10/1914
War Diary	Doulieu		31/10/1914	31/10/1914
Miscellaneous	7th Infty Bde. 3rd Bn Worcestershire Regt.			
Heading	7th Brigade. 3rd Division. Battalion attached to 8th Brigade 17th November to 3rd December 1914. 3rd Battalion Worcestershire Regiment November 1914			
Heading	7th Brigade 3rd Worcester Rgt Vol IV 1-30.11.14			
War Diary	Merris		01/11/1914	01/11/1914
War Diary	Ploegsteert		02/11/1914	02/11/1914
War Diary	Bois De Ploegsteert		03/11/1914	08/11/1914
War Diary	Ploegsteert		09/11/1914	16/11/1914
War Diary	Petit Pont		17/11/1914	17/11/1914
War Diary	Neuve Eglise		18/11/1914	19/11/1914
War Diary	La Clytte		20/11/1914	20/11/1914
War Diary	Kemmel		21/11/1914	23/11/1914
War Diary	Danoutre		24/11/1914	25/11/1914
War Diary	Lindenhoek		26/11/1914	28/11/1914
War Diary	Westoutre		29/11/1914	29/11/1914
War Diary	Locre		30/11/1914	30/11/1914
Heading	7th Brigade 3rd Division Battalion Seased to be attached to 8th Brigade 3rd December 1914 3rd Battalion Worcestershire Regiment December 1914			
Heading	7th Brigade 3rd Worcesters. Vol V 1-31.12.14			
War Diary	Locre		01/12/1914	02/12/1914
War Diary	Locre & Kemmel		03/12/1914	03/12/1914
War Diary	Westoutre		04/12/1914	05/12/1914
War Diary	Scherpenberg		06/12/1914	09/12/1914
War Diary	E Kemmel		10/12/1914	12/12/1914
War Diary	Locre		13/12/1914	14/12/1914
War Diary	E Kemmel		15/12/1914	18/12/1914
War Diary	Locre		19/12/1914	23/12/1914
War Diary	E Kemmel		24/12/1914	26/12/1914
War Diary	Westoutre		27/12/1914	30/12/1914
War Diary	Locre		31/12/1914	31/12/1914
Heading	3rd Division 7th Infy Bde 3rd Battalion Worcestershire Regt. Jan-Oct 1915			
Heading	7th Inf. Bde. 3rd Div. 3rd Battalion Worcestershire Regiment. Jan 1915			
War Diary	Locre		01/01/1915	03/01/1915
War Diary	E Kemmel		04/01/1915	07/01/1915
War Diary	Westoutre		08/01/1915	11/01/1915
War Diary	E Kemmel		13/01/1915	15/01/1915
War Diary	Westoutre		16/01/1915	19/01/1915
War Diary	E Kemmel		20/01/1915	23/01/1915
War Diary	Locre		24/01/1915	27/01/1915
War Diary	E Kemmel		28/01/1915	31/01/1915
Heading	7th Inf. Bde. 3rd Div. War Diary 3rd Battn. The Worcestershire Regiment. February 1915			
War Diary	Locre		01/02/1915	04/02/1915
War Diary	Kemmel		05/02/1915	08/02/1915
War Diary	Locre		09/02/1915	12/02/1915
War Diary	Kemmel		13/02/1915	21/02/1915
War Diary	Locre		22/02/1915	25/02/1915
War Diary	Kemmel		26/02/1915	28/02/1915

Heading	7th Inf. Bde. 3rd Div. War Diary. 3rd Battn. The Worcestershire Regiment. March 1915		
War Diary	Kemmel	01/03/1915	03/03/1915
War Diary	Locre	04/03/1915	11/03/1915
War Diary	Kemmel (Lindenhoek)	12/03/1915	12/03/1915
War Diary	Locre	13/03/1915	15/03/1915
War Diary	Kemmel	16/03/1915	18/03/1915
War Diary	La Clytte	19/03/1915	19/03/1915
War Diary	Locre	20/03/1915	22/03/1915
War Diary	Ellzenwalle	23/03/1915	28/03/1915
War Diary	La Clytte & Dickebusch	29/03/1915	31/03/1915
Miscellaneous	7th Inf. 3rd Div. 3rd Battn. War Diary The Worcestershire Regiment. April 1915		
War Diary	Dickebush	01/04/1915	03/04/1915
War Diary	E Dickebush	04/04/1915	09/04/1915
War Diary	La Clytte	10/04/1915	15/04/1915
War Diary	E Dickebush	16/04/1915	19/04/1915
War Diary	Dickebush	20/04/1915	24/04/1915
War Diary	E Dickebush	23/04/1915	29/04/1915
War Diary	Dickebush	30/04/1915	30/04/1915
Heading	7th Inf. Bde. 3rd Div. War Diary 3rd Battn. The Worcestershire Regiment. May 1915		
War Diary	Dickebush	01/05/1915	03/05/1915
War Diary	E Dickebush	04/05/1915	15/05/1915
War Diary	La Clytte	16/05/1915	19/05/1915
War Diary	E Dickebush	20/05/1915	23/05/1915
War Diary	La Clytte & Dickebush	24/05/1915	25/05/1915
War Diary	E Vierstraat	26/05/1915	31/05/1915
Heading	7th Inf. Bde. 3rd Div. War Diary 3rd Battn. The Worcestershire Regiment. June 1915		
War Diary	E. Vierstraat	01/06/1915	02/06/1915
War Diary	Dickebusch	03/06/1915	03/06/1915
War Diary	Nr. Vlamertinche	04/06/1915	04/06/1915
War Diary	Nr. Hooghe	05/06/1915	08/06/1915
War Diary	Nr. Busseboom	09/06/1915	14/06/1915
War Diary	East of Ypres near Hooghe.	15/06/1915	15/06/1915
War Diary	Hooghe	16/06/1915	30/06/1915
Heading	7th Inf. Bde. 3rd Div. War Diary 3rd Battn. The Worcestershire Regiment. July 1915		
War Diary		01/07/1915	31/07/1915
Heading	7th Inf. Bde. 3rd Div. War Diary 3rd Battn. The Worcestershire Regiment. October 1915		
War Diary		01/08/1915	30/08/1915
Heading	7th Inf. Bde. 3rd Div. War Diary 3rd Battn. The Worcestershire Regiment. September 1915		
War Diary		01/09/1915	30/09/1915
Heading	7th Inf. Bde. 3rd Div. War Diary 3rd Battn. The Worcestershire Regiment. October 1915		
War Diary		01/10/1915	31/10/1915

WO 95/1415

3 DIV 7 INFANTRY BDE

3 Battn Worcestershire Regt

Aug 1914 - Oct 1915

3RD DIVISION
7TH INFY BDE

3RD BATTALION

THE WORCESTERSHIRE REGT.

AUG - DEC 1914

7th Brigade.
3rd Division

1

3rd BATTALION

THE WORCESTERSHIRE REGIMENT

AUGUST 1 9 1 4::::::::

Miss Brown (?)

J.1

121/868

WAR DIARY.

3rd Bn. Worcestershire Regt.

— 7th Brigade.

Volume I. 4 — 31.8.14

7/3

WAR DIARY
or
INTELLIGENCE SUMMARY.
(Erase heading not required.)

Army Form C. 2118.

Instructions regarding War Diaries and Intelligence Summaries are contained in F.S. Regs., Part II. and the Staff Manual respectively. Title pages will be prepared in manuscript.

Hour, Date, Place	Summary of Events and Information	Remarks and references to Appendices
Worth 3.45 p.m. 4.8.14	Mobilization orders received.	
" 5.8.14. 10.45/9 pm	Mobilization carried out according to programme. Reinforcements arrived at 10.45 p.m.	
" 6.8.14. 10.40 p.m.	Mobilization carried out according to Programme. Arrived to offrs 9.2.16 arrived 10.40 p.m.	
" 7.8.14. 9.30 p.m.	Mobilization carried out according to Programme. Arrived to offrs 9.2.09 arrived 9.30 p.m.	
" 8.8.14. 11.5 p.m.	Mobilization carried out according to Programme. Arrived to others arrived 11.5 p.m.	
" 9.8.14	Mobilization completed with the exception of two Subaltern offrs. 9.10 p.m.	
" 10.8.14	Companies placed at the Disposal of O.C. Chaplains. In Sunday Drill	
" 11.8.14	1 Brigade Route March. (2) Capt. Maxwell (Maj. M.) at disposal of O.C. Capn.	
" 12.8.14	Capn placed at Disposal of O.C. Capn. Battalion Route March Mobilization Order 11 A.M.	
" 13.8.14	Left Worth by 2 Trains for Southampton. Arrived Southampton 7 A.M.	
Southampton 14.8.14	Left Southampton 4.45 A.M. on S.S. Borrian. Arrived off Havre 2.40 p.m.	S.S. Borrian. Very little accommodation on board, and a bit of scampering
	Lay there until 1.30 p.m. 15.8.14	
Havre 15.8.14	Left Havre for Rouen arrived Rouen 9 p.m. Remained for night on Troy	
	until 7 A.M.	
Havre 16.8.14	Left at 7 A.M. Marched to Gard de Nord Arrived 7.35 A.M. Entrained & left	
	(Arrives arrived 4.20 p.m. Left 4.46 arrived Aumoye 10.30 p.m.	
	(Strasbourg for night)	
Aumoye 17.8.14	Left at 7 A.M. for Maribaix Arrived 9 A.M. Went into Billets	
Maribaix 18.8.14	Battalion Route March 9 A.M.	
Maribaix 19.8.14	Battalion Route March 9 A.M.	
Dompierre 20.8.14	Left Maribaix 9 A.M. Went into Billets. Took part in Brigade Route March at 2.15 p.m. Went to Avesnes, returning to Billets 6.44 p.m.	

WAR DIARY
or
INTELLIGENCE SUMMARY.
(Erase heading not required.)

Army Form C. 2118.

Instructions regarding War Diaries and Intelligence Summaries are contained in F. S. Regs., Part II. and the Staff Manual respectively. Title pages will be prepared in manuscript.

Hour, Date, Place	Summary of Events and Information	Remarks and references to Appendices
21-8-14 FEIGNIES		
22-8-14	Bombardiers	
23-8-14	Left DOMPIERE 5.15 AM and marched via Thy to FEIGNIE'S arrived 12 noon at Village and went into billets.	
24-8-14	Marched to CIPLY and went into Bivac. CIPLY. Noisy night about 12.30 pm & 6 A.M. up & Reheated. 17 Fusilier Brigade Bde on right. The Watering at Rifle ∴ Machine gun Rear - bivouaced in billets. CIPLY - Detailed in early orchards & fell back through BAAY and retd up hill at outposts along railway line about HALTE. R. I. Rifles on our left.	Casualties 2 killed (Bowman?) 11 missing
25-8-14	Still heard from HALTE. B. buy over toward BEAUGRAND. RIFLES Brought LE QUESNOY - VOLEMIES to CAUDREY. Covered by WILTSHIRE Regt. R. I. Rifles. - Went into billets at CAUDREY about 10 p.m.	
26-8-14	Occupied two trenches on W & NW of town about 2.30 a.m. with two companies - attacked early morning & 13 cent? & engines on N.W. W & N - Very heavy & skillful. Especially to the Northern most trenches portions of W. Regt. - Vacated village about 2 p.m. but returned & reoccupied it again as far as MARKET SQUARE with advanced parties on N. & NW. W.B. about 1 hour later. Finally evacuated it about 4.30 p.m. Retired via MONTIGNY - CLARY - ELINCOURT, MALINCOURT to BEAUVOIS.	8 killed 12 wounded (17 missing) LT. CLARKE killed MAJ CHICHESTER severely wounded dang. Capt BERNISTON? dang. Capt ELLIOTT Lt. UNDERHILL slightly Lt. LEE missing

79
3298

WAR DIARY
or
INTELLIGENCE SUMMARY.

(Erase heading not required.)

Army Form C. 2118.

Instructions regarding War Diaries and Intelligence Summaries are contained in F.S. Regs., Part II. and the Staff Manual respectively. Title pages will be prepared in manuscript.

Hour, Date, Place	Summary of Events and Information	Remarks and references to Appendices
27-8-12	Moved at 3 a.m. via ESTRÉES, AGICOURT, VILLAREY to VERMAND. Took up covering posit'n and remained till relieved by R Scott Fusiliers at 8.30 pm. Travelled at 10.17 p.m. via HAM to TAREFESSE - to BILLETS at TAREFESSE.	
28-8-12		
29-8-12	Left TARLFESSE 3 p.m. and marched to VALENCY & took up outpost position with right resting on R. OISE & left at DOMINOIS - WILSTONE. Rest at 11 p.m. - at 10 p.m. relieved by W. Lt. Regt & ordered to take up line from ½ South N W. of TARLFESSE to GENVRY - or arrived at NOYON skipped Rest by Tarlton & Pro Meiind	
30-8-12	Left NOYON 2.30 a.m. forming rearguard to 3rd Div'n - arrived Vic sur AISNE 6 p.m. went into BIVC.	
31-8-12	Left Vic sur AISNE 7 a.m. marched via MONTEFONTAINE - VIVIERES - TAILLEFONTAINE - EMEVILLE to COYOLLES - Rearguard to Div'n (3rd) Went into Bivouac in CHATEAU COYOLLES PARK.	

25-9-14

7th Brigade.
3rd Division.

3rd BATTALION

WORCESTERSHIRE REGIMENT

SEPTEMBER 1914:

Mrs West

J.2

121/1084

3rd Worcestershire Regt.
7th Brigade
Volume II. 1—30.9.14

re organisation & equipment.

WAR DIARY
or
INTELLIGENCE SUMMARY.
(Erase heading not required.)

Army Form C. 2118.

Instructions regarding War Diaries and Intelligence Summaries are contained in F.S. Regs., Part II. and the Staff Manual respectively. Title pages will be prepared in manuscript.

Hour, Date, Place	Summary of Events and Information	Remarks and references to Appendices
COYOLLES 1st Sep 7.30 am	Marched via LEVIGNEN to FRESNOY.	
2 am. 2nd Sept.	Marched via FOSSE MARTIN, DOUY to MARCILLY. Hadn't been used up day. In evening took up outpost line with WILTSHIRE Regt on general line 1/2 mile N BARCY — ST SOUPPLETS — (WILTS on right - WORCESTERSHIRE on left).	
4. a.m. 3rd Sept S¹ SOUPPLETS	Outpost - at 7.30 am at 9 am to PRINCY - Marched thence 9 a.m. via MEAUX to NANCY and went into bivouac at NANCY	
4 Sept NANCY		
11 pm 4 Sept NANCY	Marched via CRECY to LES CHAPELLES BOURBON. Furnished outpost on the Train Station - CHAMPROISE FARM - 1 Coy [?] Reinforcements joined Battalion under Lieut. Pitchingrill Cunliffe	
5-14 LES CHAPELLES BOURBON 6th Sep		
5. a.m. LES CHAPELLES BOURBON 7 Sep	Marched via OBELISQUE FAVIEMONT at FAROUTTIERS.	
9. 26 am. FAROUTTIERS 7 Sept.	Our Company (C) left at 9.25 am Rapport N. Lam Regt at St AUGUSTIN. Return about 3 p.m. Left + right 5-30 pm ant Bivouaced at LES PETITS AULNOIS — Batt⁹ on offset duty.	
7.35 am 8th Sept LES PETITS AULNOIS	Marched at 7.35 am via CHAUFFRY. Found up at LAROYERE Preparatory to forcing R. JOANNE. Bivouaced at BUSSIERE.	

WAR DIARY
or
INTELLIGENCE SUMMARY.

(Erase heading not required.)

Army Form C. 2118.

Instructions regarding War Diaries and Intelligence Summaries are contained in F.S. Regs., Part II. and the Staff Manual respectively. Title pages will be prepared in manuscript.

Hour, Date, Place	Summary of Events and Information	Remarks and references to Appendices
7.31 9" Sep! BUSSIERES	Left Bussieres at 7.31 a.m. and (10.30) ROANNE. Halt for some Time awaiting other Columns. Other into from (?)	
10" Sep! MONTEMAFROY	10.05 MONTEMAFROY.	
5.00 11" Sep! MONTEMAFROY	Left 5.00 11" Sep! at GRAND ROZOY.	
9 am 12" Sep! CERSEUIL	Left MONTEMAFROY 9 am 12" (Brigade attack with 8" Bde in CERSEUIL. But on arrival only Enemy CERSEUIL - Pouring wet night	
7.30 13" Sep! BRAINE	Left CERSEUIL 7.30 a.m. on reaching BRAINE (Batt". dispos!) in Reserve 5E 4 p.m. then into Bivouac N.E. of BRAINE.	
5 pm. 14" Sep! VAILLY	Moved off 5 am & marched in Rd to G- CHATEAU CHASSEMY For road broad. - Heavily Shelled on Town & Chateau in road some L.NS BaleR and six other rank. Sent two companies (A v B) across river by pontoons in support, with 2/Y.L.R/The at 4 p.m. Remaining two companies moved about 9 pm – 2/S.W. attack at E of BUCY. – 13" Sep! went to VAILLY by pontoon bridge. Two Companies (A v C) A & B support 2/A.Y. Lord R/The "C" R/Lyers at Valley Reg! moved up A.T.T" a my. Bent in Bivouac – 13" B. D. Bat in reserve in billets and). Shares the Hos 113 - Had 4 th woo'ed about open to 7.30 pm 2 hours 9 a.m. 13 pm 13" (R.D. Rifles.) 9.7 & 8.12 Entrenched across valley N. ORIGNIAL.	

WAR DIARY
or
INTELLIGENCE SUMMARY.

(Erase heading not required.)

Army Form C. 2118.

Instructions regarding War Diaries and Intelligence Summaries are contained in F.S. Regs., Part II. and the Staff Manual respectively. Title pages will be prepared in manuscript.

Hour, Date, Place	Summary of Events and Information	Remarks and references to Appendices
Trenches	posts at N. end of valley by farm. Some firing about midnight but no real attack. Casualties 2 killed, 25 wounded, 3 missing.	
16th Sept. VAILLY	In same position. Very heavy shelling in morning about 9 a.m. & later. Expt. Westminsters. Shelling throughout the day. Casualties 7 killed & 9 wounded.	
17th Sept. Trenches VAILLY	Shelling from 5 a.m. throughout day. At times very heavy. Captain BORMAN & 6 wounded.	
18th Sept. Trenches VAILLY	Intermittent & at times heavy shelling all day. Casualties 1 wounded & 1 missing.	
19th Sept. Trenches VAILLY	Rather heavy rifle & heavy shelling at day. Attack a hostile attack 5-30 p.m. Casualties 1 killed 12 wounded.	
20 Sept. Trenches VAILLY	Firing commenced at dawn & heavy shelling all the morning. Attack at 12.15 (?) where it. It was destroying German hotel through 2 round rifle March 9 Brigade Capt. Dorsen cut. Casualties Lieut: C. HENRY, Lieut H. T. G. GILMOUR,	

WAR DIARY
or
INTELLIGENCE SUMMARY.

(Erase heading not required.)

Army Form C. 2118.

Hour, Date, Place	Summary of Events and Information	Remarks and references to Appendices
21st Sept. Trenches VAILLY	2 Lieut. C.C. HARRISON killed & 31 killed, 2 Lt. T.P MUSPRATT & 37 wounded, and about 30 missing. Some shelling about midday otherwise quiet day. (Casualties 2 officers)	
22nd " CHANNEMY	Relieved at midnight 21/22 by 2/LEICESTERSHIRE Regt. & moved into bivouac about 2 miles N. of BRAINE. Left 3.30 p.m and moved to CHASSEMY and relieved NORFOLK Regt. on N. of BRAINE - VAILLY road on outpost covering CHASSEMY and watching CONDÉ Bridge.	
23rd Sept CHANNEMY	Occupying same position as on 22nd	
24 Sept CHASSEMY	Relieved at 7 p.m. by 2/S. LANC. Regt. & moved into billets at AUGY.	
25th Sept AUGY	At AUGY in billets	
26th Sept AUGY	At AUGY in billets.	

Army Form C. 2118.

WAR DIARY
or
INTELLIGENCE SUMMARY.
(Erase heading not required.)

Hour, Date, Place	Summary of Events and Information	Remarks and references to Appendices
27th Sept. AUBY.	Entrained from 7 to 13.30 a.m. directing 13e Rolland Franne. 3.20 a.m. orders to march at once via LA GRANGE FARM to BOIS ANCIENNES on report of enemy's crossing of GIRONNO by CONDE Bridge. Report false & Bgde returned to Billets at AUBY 6 P.m. - 10.30 a.m.	
28th Sept AUBY	Message received 5.40 a.m. to turn at once to BOIS ANCIENNES in reserve. Moved off 6.15 a.m. Arrived at position 7.0 a.m. Returned to Billets at AUBY at 10 a.m. Arrived 11.15 a.m.	
29th Sept. AUBY	In Billets at AUBY.	
30th Sept AUBY	In Billets at AUBY.	

R.W.R. Read Lt Colonel
Comdg 3 Worcester Regt Bgd.

1st Lt. Wm.

7th Brigade.

3rd Division.

3rd BATTALION

WORCESTERSHIRE REGIMENT

OCTOBER 1 9 1 4

121/2306

3rd Worcestershire Regt.
7th Brigade.
Vol III. 1 - 31.10.14

WAR DIARY
or
INTELLIGENCE SUMMARY.
(Erase heading not required.)

Army Form C. 2118.

Instructions regarding War Diaries and Intelligence Summaries are contained in F.S. Regs., Part II. and the Staff Manual respectively. Title pages will be prepared in manuscript.

Hour, Date, Place	Summary of Events and Information	Remarks and references to Appendices
3.30am 1st Oct. AUGY	Left AUGY 4 retired 9/units on enquête. Lived at CHASSEMY.	
2nd Oct. CHASSEMY	54th Bay outpost - Line at CHASSEMY. 10th Hussars retired 13th at 7.30pm. 13th Hussars retired to GRAND ROZOY	
5am 3rd Oct. GRAND ROZOY	The whole GRAND ROZOY went into Bivouac. Marched at 5.30 pm by other route to LA FERTE MILON to Bivouac at COYOLLES. King Flurry Knight absent.	?
4.30am 5th Oct. COYOLLES	Arrived COYOLLES. Day in Bivouac - Marched at 8.30pm with 4.3rd 13th R.F.A. to Bivouac VAINTIMES.	
12 noon 6th Oct. VAINTIMES	Left VAINTIMES for PONT ST MAXENCE. Arrived 3.45am entrained. Diff. 4,200 men left by train (cattle trucks throughout) Reinforcement of 13th with transport left by train at 12.45pm. Inactivity at PICQUIGNY. [Train reached in rating during night at PICQUIGNY] (Sent)	
1.45 pm 7th Oct. PIERVIANT	Left by train at 1.30 pm — Arr. PONT REMY 2.30 pm. Detrained & marched out at 4.30pm to Billet 21st LE PLESSIER. 1st Hus (less Mar Ext) Joined 13th Hus & 7th Brigade (much at 7.) There.	
8th Oct. LE PLESSIER	No. 1. 8h. 9th Oct. LE PLESSIER.	
12.25am 9th Oct. LE PLESSIER	Marched at 12.25 am. to MEANVILLE - arrived 8 am prev. W. Billets. Left 4.5 pm for PERNES. Marched to HESDIN. Thence by whole train. A.m. out 12.30 am. Went to Billets.	
5/04. 10th Oct. PERNES	Billets R.1. Rifles in outposts at 6.7am.	

WAR DIARY
or
INTELLIGENCE SUMMARY
(Erase heading not required.)

Army Form C. 2118.

Instructions regarding War Diaries and Intelligence Summaries are contained in F. S. Regs, Part II. and the Staff Manual respectively. Title pages will be prepared in manuscript.

Hour, Date, Place	Summary of Events and Information	Remarks and References to Appendices
9 am. 11th Oct. RENNES.	Detrained at 9 am. 13th Great sub: B.Bde. at LANNOY just E. of GONNEHEM at 9/pm. [Remainder 7th Brigade at HINGES]	
7.15 am. 12th Oct. LANNOY	Marched 9 7th & 13th Brigade at HINGES taken to LACOUTRE. Shelljo Huis de 678: 13th Corps Carried concerted against RICHEBOURG ST VAAST. Half of 7th Bde Div. in echelon here for the right. 7th Brigade From just E LACOUTRE to point about ½ mile W. of R. in RICHEBOURG L'AVOUÉ.	Casualties: Captain ELLIOTT L.t C. NOTTLEY 2 Lieut CRAW KEITH, Cyril NASERBY & Lt C. TYSON V 20 N.C.O. men wounded — 8 Rank & File missing —
5.30 am 13th Oct till LACOUTRE	Sent out patrols & by dawn had 2 Companies occupying RICHEBOURG ST VAAST. — Supported them later by remainder of Batt.n — Entrenched during the night — N. LANC. Regt. on our left, E. SURREY Regt. on our right.	1 Rank & File killed, 5 wounded 2 missing
14th Oct. RICHEBOURG ST VAAST	S. Sunday at RICHEBOURG ST VAAST. Shelling at intervals — yeo Munster our one Commander killed — Night attack about 6.30 pm. 2 on his right heavy firing during night	Rank & File 2 killed 6 wounded
15th Oct. RICHEBOURG ST VAAST.	Sunday.	Capt. T HUGHES killed, Capt N P.T JEFFERIES, 2 L.T PRITCHARD wounded — Rank & File 10 killed 20 wounded
16th Oct. RICHEBOURG ST VAAST.	Advanced via ST. VAAST to x roads N.E. of NEUVE CHAPELLE, thence through BOIS DE BIEZ & occupied line N.E. Pte	Rank & File 1 wounded 2 L'T LEE wounded.

WAR DIARY or INTELLIGENCE SUMMARY

Army Form C. 2118.

Hour, Date, Place	Summary of Events and Information	Remarks and References to Appendices
17th Oct: BOIS DE BIEZ	Advanced - Halted for some time just E. of HERLIES RANGE. The offensive slowed further advance against what was evidently another night fire. - Half gn at LE HUE. Night quiet. Extended to B Coys.	2 L' HASTINGS, MEDHURST KIM'd Pat. & L'L. & Kelth.
5 a.m. 18th Oct: LE HUE	Relieved by W KENT Reg.t at 3 a.m. Reports as at writing. Went into billets at PONT LOGY. Heavy fire 5.30 am then moved to BERK [?] just W of BOIS DE BIEZ.	
6 a.m. 19th Oct: BOIS DE BIEZ	Occupied E. edge of BOIS DE BIEZ at 6 a.m. Remained till 12 noon when relieved to billets.	
2.15 am 20th Oct: do.	Left billets at 2.15 am and occupied N line of trenches at LE HUE - Mainly missed by enemy in afternoon - Humphries & Rank & Wk 2 bn 16.d. 10 LANCS on my right with patrol - Enfilade and at last remained unionless - of L.L. Ancs Reg.t came up supplied up W KENT Reg.t on West. Throughout period fog by night.	2nd & 2 L' F R HARVEY wounded -
7 a.m. 21st Oct: LE HUE	Enemy attacked in foggy morning & where troops took line of Dry H Cavalry 2 Platoon a. My of NORF Reg.t & Ham & Many HERTS. Again & 13th Bn DLI on bat 6.9 Gradually Staff took on 6 Lunt of LE HUE Salient - At noon occupied Trench where Fac'd Line Temporarily vacated T. enquired of ground could retake wounded - Rand i St. K 2nd 13 T. 3 wounded - 29 Missing of N LONE Reg. & N W KENT Reg. 1- to SW of to W LE HUE.	1 st W A UNDERHILL 2nd L' E C V BATTLE, L' GALTON KIMG, Cap.t E. L. D. BROWNELL 2 LT. C. WYNTER 2Lt. CARPENDALE, Cap.t P.S. STUART.

WAR DIARY or INTELLIGENCE SUMMARY

Army Form C. 2118.

Hour, Date, Place	Summary of Events and Information	Remarks and References to Appendices
F.E. Stopford	and about 200 yards N. of the Le Hue – Longues road. Pushed out another company (B) at Road X 1857 on the Chine pinching a new line being taken up by Bde.	
4.30 am 22nd Oct: LE HUE	On 22nd line being taken up by R. Rifles, Wilts Regt & R.W. Kent Regt with Rens to positions N of 1807 OS 13152 – Bn J Zouave & 2nd Lt Pickersgill Conlisse wounded – Rank & File 18 killed Battn. mvd to Rue Marais N.E. of Richebourg L'Avoue – at 12 noon 13 wounded K.127 moved to Co. B – inferior O.C.F.B inferred to Rue du Marais – subsequently remainder 137 conc'd up. Attack which was made in conjunction with Manchester attack from right front made the of Rue du Marais –	
12m & 1am. 23rd Oct: RUE DU MARAIS	This has occupied during night 13th covered by rear guard & posted in neighbourhood of La Quinque Rue. Brigade at Le Cornett Malherbe – some fatigue.	Rank & File 1 killed 3 wounded
24th LA QUINQUE RUE	In trenches – preparing & strengthening entrenchments.	Rank & File 3 wounded 1 sentry
25th LA QUINQUE RUE	Very heavy sniping of killing – During night enemy advanced trench & blown trigger.	Rank & File 1 killed, 1 wounded 1 sentry
26th LA QUINQUE RUE	Enemy sniped all day – attacked up ditches towards Manchester Rgt. War a fire & firing scene exploded front of Rue du Bois. No one hurt.	Rank & File 7 wounded
27th LA QUINQUE RUE	Enemy attacked between our & 10am. attack chiefly directed against Manchesters and Lr. Drive of & 1.30am. Repulsed by L. Drives nowhere.	Rank & File 6 killed 10 wounded.

WAR DIARY
or
INTELLIGENCE SUMMARY
(Erase heading not required.)

Army Form C. 2118

Instructions regarding War Diaries and Intelligence Summaries are contained in F. S. Regs., Part II. and the Staff Manual respectively. Title pages will be prepared in manuscript.

Hour, Date, Place	Summary of Events and Information	Remarks and References to Appendices
27th Oct. LA QUINQUE RUE (cca:)	Very easy shelling during day.	Rank & File 6 killed 10 wounded.
28th Oct. LA QUINQUE RUE	A violent night. Attacks at sunset, 3.30 a.m. and dawn. but attack with javelins. Artillery commenced 7 a.m. Artillery (enemy) found range. A Co.'s night bombers & provided few moments during night attack about 9.30 p.m. – not pushed. Otherwise night turns on two sides.	Rank & File 1 killed 6 wounded.
4.30a.m 29th Oct. LA QUINQUE RUE.	Heavy rifle fire about 6.20 a.m. – Causing some damage to A Co. trenches. Followed afterwards by infantry attack from front. Germans advanced to a rest. Then against wire trenches – whilst night firing at along two counter attacks.	Rank & File 2 killed 1/15 wounded.
2 a.m. 30th Oct. LA QUINQUE RUE	Relieved in trenches by LEICESTERSHIRE Regt and marched to BETHUNE en route. Stores at 12 noon marched to [L]ACOUTRE & joined 7th Brigade – marched at 2.30 pm. to BETHUNE at DOULIEU.	Rank & File 1 killed 3 wounded 1 missing
9 a.m. 31st Oct. DOULIEU	Marched to MERRIS & billeted in billets.	

18.11.14

B.W.M. The Lieutenant
2nd Gloucestershire Regt

4th Infy Bde 3rd Bn Worcestershire Regt

Date	Officers Killed	Officers Wounded	Officers Missing	Other Ranks Killed	Other Ranks Wounded	Other Ranks Missing
12.10.14	Lt R Northey, Capt H R Elliott	Capt C Mainwaring		15	20	5
13.10.14		2/Lt C Tycorn				2
14.10.14				1	5	
15.10.14	Capt F H Hughes	2/Lt F Pritchard, Capt H A J Jefferies		2	6	
16.10.14				4	20	
17.10.14		2/Lt R H M Lee		2		
18.10.14	2/Lt J L Harley-Rathurst	2/Lt F B Harvey			1	1
20.10.14	Lt-Col W Rindrotoll, 2/Lt E C E Backe, Lt Eyerham	Capt E J B Brownell, Lt K C Winter, 2/Lt S-J Scarfoundale, Capt R B Stewart x		2	10	
21.10.14				13	23	29

x R.A.M.C.

3rd Bn Worcestershire Regt

Date	Killed	Officers Wounded	Missing	Killed (Other Ranks)	Wounded	Missing
22.10.14	7			38	140	39
23.10.14					13	
24.10.14		1 Lt Cunliffe		4	5	1
25.10.14					3	
26.10.14					7	
27.10.14					4	
27.10.14				6	10	
28.10.14			Includes 1 R.A.M.C.	1	6	15
29.10.14				4		–
	7	1		54	213	40

7th Brigade.
3rd Division.

Battalion attached to 8th Brigade
17th November to 3rd December 1914.

3rd BATTALION

WORCESTERSHIRE REGIMENT

NOVEMBER 1 9 1 4

7th Brigade.
3rd Division.

Battalion attached to 8th Brigade
17th November to 3rd December 1914.

3rd BATTALION

WORCESTERSHIRE REGIMENT

NOVEMBER 1914

M67

3/7?

7th Brigade
2nd Worcester Regt.

Vol IV. 1-30.11.14

$\frac{121}{2650}$

$\frac{121}{2650}$

Nov 1st 16th
attached THIRD CORPS

Nov. 17th - 30th
attached 8th Bde

WAR DIARY
or
INTELLIGENCE SUMMARY
(Erase heading not required.)

Army Form C. 2118.

Instructions regarding War Diaries and Intelligence Summaries are contained in F. S. Regs., Part II. and the Staff Manual respectively. Title pages will be prepared in manuscript.

Hour, Date, Place	Summary of Events and Information	Remarks and References to Appendices
		3/29
7 a.m. 1st Nov. MENIN	Orders received. The imperial France et Shot cable.	
10.25 a.m. do.	Bn's moved in motor busses to NEUVE EGLISE. On arrival went into A.H.Q. Moved at 3 p.m. via POPERINGHE to Divonne W. of PLOEGSTEERT, relieving one Company (D) to support R.I./E.LANC. REST AT LE GHIER.	
6 a.m. 2nd Nov. PLOEGSTEERT	Moved Bn's. two coys Company to position just W of BOIS DE PLOEGSTEERT. At dusk moved up and relieved HAMPSHIRE REGT in trenches – 137 O.R. in fire trenches A. & C. in support trenches.	Casualties 1 Rank & File wounded.
3rd Nov. BOIS DE PLOEGSTEERT	In trenches – Some shelling in company heavy shelling in rear (between 4 pm & 7 pm) of trenches.	2 Lt. C. F. MOORE wounded Rank & File 6 killed 16 wounded
4 Nov. BOIS DE PLOEGSTEERT	In trenches. Some shelling about 1.30 pm. Otherwise quiet day. Heavy rain 10pm – 1 am.	
5th Nov. BOIS DE PLOEGSTEERT	In trenches. Heavy shelling and a lot of sniping of trenches.	Rank & File 3 killed 6 wounded
6th Nov. BOIS DE PLOEGSTEERT	In trenches – Again heavy shelling of trenches.	Cases W^so 6th 7th of L.
7th Nov. BOIS DE PLOEGSTEERT	Between 3 am – 7 am very heavy bombardment of front trenches. Very heavy fog during which at 6 had 3 am enemy broke through right of trenches of B.C. Co. Efforts made through day with assistance of INNISKILLING FUSRS, EAST LANC. REGT & one Company SEAFORTH HIGHLANDERS to dislodge them but unsuccessfully.	Killed Captain A.S. NESBITT Lieut J.B. VANZELEUR " J.A. GOLDSMID " J.M. ATKIN Wounded " H.C. MILWARD 2/Lieut H. STOCKLEY

79
3298

Army Form C. 2118.

WAR DIARY
or
INTELLIGENCE SUMMARY
(Erase heading not required.)

Instructions regarding War Diaries and Intelligence Summaries are contained in F. S. Regs., Part II. and the Staff Manual respectively. Title pages will be prepared in manuscript.

Hour, Date, Place	Summary of Events and Information	Remarks and References to Appendices
8th Nov. BOIS DE PLOEGSTEERT	In Trenches. Sniping & Shelling during day. In evening Batt. relieved by ARGYLL & SUTHERLAND Hrs in centre, E. LANC: on right, 7 LANC: FUSRS on left, and returned to Billets N of PLOEGSTEERT	Rank & File Killed 4, 2 Wounded 12, 1 Missing 39 3/29 ot
9th Nov. PLOEGSTEERT	2.20 pm. Machine gun Sect: to Trenches with E. LANC: Reg"al. Batt: moved out of Billets at 11 pm.	
10th Nov. PLOEGSTEERT	Relieved to Billets at 5.30 am.	
11th Nov. PLOEGSTEERT	Furnished working parties Support communication Through BOIS DE ROESTEERT	Rank & File 2 wounded
12th Nov. PLOEGSTEERT	In Billets at PLOEGSTEERT	
13th Nov. PLOEGSTEERT	In Billets at PLOEGSTEERT. One Company (A) sent out Support Hants in support. HAMPSHIRE REGT.	Rank & File 1 wounded
14th Nov. PLOEGSTEERT	3 Coys in Billets at PLOEGSTEERT. 6 pm Took over fire trenches No1/2 Coy (D & 1/2 B) from SOMERSETSHIRE L. INF. 1/2 Coy in Reserve Trenches to RIFLE BRIGADE	
15th Nov. PLOEGSTEERT	In Trenches as on 14th.	
16th Nov. PLOEGSTEERT	In Trenches as on 15th. Relieved by RIFLE BRIGADE, (3 Coys), and by 10 pm. and marched to Billets at PETIT PONT.	

WAR DIARY
or
INTELLIGENCE SUMMARY
(Erase heading not required.)

Army Form C. 2118.

Instructions regarding War Diaries and Intelligence Summaries are contained in F. S. Regs., Part II. and the Staff Manual respectively. Title pages will be prepared in manuscript.

Hour, Date, Place	Summary of Events and Information	Remarks and References to Appendices
5.30 a.m. 17th Nov: PETIT PONT	Oct Co: (A) rejoined at PETIT PONT from support trenches to HAMPSHIRE WEST of PLOEGSTEERT. Bett. (marched) & arrived at NEUVE EGLISE at 9. a.m. Paris attached to 10th Brigade. Went into billets. One Company (C) centered at 8 p.m. to relieve to DOZEN R.F. E.P. WULVERGHEM — Relieved 6 a.m. 18th	
18th Nov: NEUVE EGLISE	One Co. (B) NEUVE EGLISE — Oct Company at 8 p.m. to relieve to DOZEN Rgt — Relieved 6 a.m. 19th	
19th Nov: NEUVE EGLISE	Received orders 2.45 p.m. to move to LOCRE at 3.30 p.m. Destination subsequently changed to LA CLYTTE. Marched there. 2 Co's STRONG 2 Co's (13 & D) to relieve trenches E. of KEMMEL in support 2nd Cav: Division	3/2 & 9
20th Nov: LA CLYTTE.	Head Qrs. & 2 Co's (A & C) moved to just N. KEMMEL at 4 p.m.	
21st Nov: KEMMEL.	at KEMMEL. Van on in Reserve trenches 2 on LM.G.	
22nd Nov: KEMMEL	As at 21st	Rank & file 2 wounds.
23rd Nov: KEMMEL	Relieved at 11 p.m. by MUNSTER FUSRS marched at 1 a.m. 24th arriving b'pacs W. DANOUTRE at 3 a.m. & attached to A 13th	
24th Nov: DANOUTRE	In billets W. DANOUTRE.	
25th Nov: DANOUTRE	Relieved D.C.L.I. in trenches E. of LINDENHOEK at 8 p.m.	
26th Nov: LINDENHOEK	In trenches. Coms: Shelling	Rank & file 2 wounded.

WAR DIARY
or
INTELLIGENCE SUMMARY

(Erase heading not required.)

Army Form C. 2118.

Hour, Date, Place	Summary of Events and Information	Remarks and References to Appendices
27th Nov. LINDENHOEK	Sn hutted E. LINDENHOEK. — Some shelling of hutters.	Rank & File 1 Killed 3 wounded
28th Nov. LINDENHOEK	In hutted E. LINDENHOEK. 1 Relieved by BEDFORDSHIRE REG.T marched to WESTOUTRE and billeted in Farm S. atttached to 15th Brigade	Rank & File 1 Killed 3 wounded
29th Nov. WESTOUTRE	In billets at WESTOUTRE.	
30th Nov. LOCRE	Marched with 15th Brigade to billets at LOCRE.	3/79 A

2.12.14

W.H. Rue Lyttleton
Col. 1. Devonshire Regt.

7th Brigade.
3rd Division.

Battalion seased to be attached to
8th Brigade 3rd December 1914.

3rd BATTALION

WORCESTERSHIRE REGIMENT

DECEMBER 1 9 1 4

T.5

121/3907

7th Brigade
3rd Worcester.
Vol V. 1 – 31.12.14

INTELLIGENCE SUMMARY

(Erase heading not required.)

Hour, Date, Place	Summary of Events and Information	Remarks and References to Appendices
1st December LOCRE.	In billets at LOCRE	
2nd " "	Three Companies marched at 3.45 p.m. to relieve Middlesex Regt N. of KEMMEL	
3rd " LOCRE KEMMEL	Three Companies N. KEMMEL. One Company (A) at LOCRE. This Company paraded for visit by H.M. the King — Companies at KEMMEL relieved by 8th Brigade. Batt. then concentrated in billets at WESTOUTRE & returned 7th Brigade.	3/29
4th " WESTOUTRE	In billets at WESTOUTRE	
5th " do	do	
6th " SCHERPENBERG	Moved to billets at SCHERPENBERG	
7th " do	In billets SCHERPENBERG	
8th " do	do	
9th " do	Retired ? to N. from ? in Trenches E. of KEMMEL	
10th " E. KEMMEL	In Trenches E. KEMMEL	Rank & File 1 killed, 2 wounded
11th " do	do	do 2 do
12th " do	do — Relieved 9.30 p.m. by Royal Scots?	do 1 do
13th " LOCRE	and marched to billets at LOCRE. In billets at LOCRE	do 1 killed

INTELLIGENCE SUMMARY

(Erase heading not required.)

Summaries are contained in F. S. Regs., Part II.
and the Staff Manual respectively. Title pages
will be prepared in manuscript.

Hour, Date, Place		Summary of Events and Information	Remarks and References to Appendices
14th December	LOCRE	Le P.M 6 at LOCRE	
15th	E. KEMMEL	Relieved 7th Hrs. in trenches E. KEMMEL 8 p.m.	Rank & file 3 wounded
16th	do	In trenches E. KEMMEL	do 3 wounded
17th	do	In trenches E. KEMMEL	do 2 wounded
18th	do	Relieved in trenches 10 p.m. by Suffolk Regt. marched to LOCRE at LOCRE	
19th	LOCRE	Le Billets at LOCRE	
20th	do	do	
21st	do	do	
22nd	do	do	
23rd	do	do	
24th	E. KEMMEL	Relieved Royal Fusiliers in trenches E. KEMMEL 8 p.m.	Rank & file 2 wounded
25th	do	In trenches E. KEMMEL	
26th	do	In trenches E. KEMMEL	do 1 wounded
27th	WESTOUTRE	Relieved at 7 p.m. in trenches by ROYAL SCOTS and SUFFOLK REGT. marched to Billets at WESTOUTRE	do 4 wounded
28th	do	In Billets WESTOUTRE	
29th	do	do	
30th	do	do	
31st	LOCRE	Marched out 4.45 p.m. to Billets at LOCRE	

1st January '15

R.T.D. MacP. Riddell
Comdg. 3/London Territorial Regt.

3RD DIVISION
7TH INFY BDE

3RD BATTALION
WORCESTERSHIRE REGT.
JAN - OCT 1915

To 25 DIV   7 BDE

7th Inf.Bde.
3rd Div.

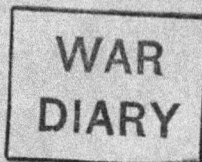

3rd BATTN. THE WORCESTERSHIRE REGIMENT.

J A N U A R Y

1 9 1 5

Army Form C. 2118.

WAR DIARY
or
INTELLIGENCE SUMMARY

(Erase heading not required.)

Instructions regarding War Diaries and Intelligence Summaries are contained in F. S. Regs., Part II. and the Staff Manual respectively. Title pages will be prepared in manuscript.

Hour, Date, Place		Summary of Events and Information	Remarks and References to Appendices
1st January '15	LOCRE	In trenches at LOCRE.	
2nd	"	do	
3rd	"	do	
4th	E. KEMMEL	do	
5th	"	Relieved Royal Fus.rs in trenches E. KEMMEL.	
6th	"	In trenches E. of KEMMEL	
7th	"	do	Rank & File. 1 wounded.
8th	WESTOUTRE	do	" 2 killed, 1 wounded.
		Relieved in trenches by Liverpool Scottish in trenches to bt Bns at WESTOUTRE	" 1 wounded.
		arriving 10 pm.	
9th	"	In billets at WESTOUTRE	
10th	"	do	
11th	"	do	
12th	E. KEMMEL	Relieved Liverpool Scottish & Det. of Royal Fus.rs & Lincolnshire Regt in	Rank & File 1 killed, 2 wounded
13th	"	trenches E. KEMMEL.	
14th	"	In trenches E. KEMMEL	" 1 " 1 "
15th	"	do	" 1 " 1 "
16th	"	do	" 1 " — "
17th	WESTOUTRE	Relieved by L. Scottish, Scott Fus.rs, Lincolns. Marched to billets at WESTOUTRE	" 2 " — "
18th	"	In billets at WESTOUTRE	
19th	"	do	
20th	E. KEMMEL	Relieved L. Scottish, Scott Fus.rs & Lincolns in trenches E. KEMMEL	

Army Form C. 2118.

WAR DIARY
or
INTELLIGENCE SUMMARY
(Erase heading not required.)

Instructions regarding War Diaries and Intelligence Summaries are contained in F. S. Regs., Part II. and the Staff Manual respectively. Title pages will be prepared in manuscript.

Hour, Date, Place		Summary of Events and Information	Remarks and References to Appendices
21st January '15	E. KEMMEL	In trenches E. KEMMEL.	Ran'ts 1/72– h:th'd 2 wounded
22nd	"	"	
23rd	"	"	" " 1 "
24th	LOCRE	Relieved by Scott Fusrs & Liverpool Scottish Tcwrnd.d 17. W.k. at LOCRE.	
25th	"	In billets at LOCRE.	
26th	"	do	
27th	"	do	
28th	E. KEMMEL	Relieved Royal Fusrs in trenches	" " 1 " 2
29th	"	In trenches E. KEMMEL	" " 1 " 1
30th	"	do	" " 1 " 4
31st	"	do	" " 1 " —

5th Feb. '15 —

7 K 19 W

R.F.W. Max?, Lieut
Cmd'g 3 Worcester Fire Reg.t

7th Inf.Bde.
3rd Div.

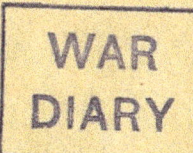

3rd BATTN. THE WORCESTERSHIRE REGIMENT.

F E B R U A R Y

1 9 1 5

Army Form C. 2118.

WAR DIARY
or
INTELLIGENCE SUMMARY
(Erase heading not required.)

Instructions regarding War Diaries and Intelligence Summaries are contained in F. S. Regs., Part II. and the Staff Manual respectively. Title pages will be prepared in manuscript.

Hour, Date, Place		Summary of Events and Information	Remarks and References to Appendices
1st Feb. 1915	LOCRE	Relieved in trenches by R Fusiliers & marched N.Trches at LOCRE	1 Rank & File wounded
2nd	"	Ln 4 Trches at LOCRE	
3rd	"	do	
4th	"	do	1 Rank & File wounded
5th	KEMMEL	Relieved Royal Fusiliers in 6 trenches E KEMMEL	3 killed 2 wounded (Rank & File)
6th	"	In Trenches E KEMMEL	3 " 2 "
7th	"	Relieved in E Trches by K.O.S.B and moved 16th Battn Trenches H A E	
8th	"	In Trches	
9th	LOCRE	Relieved by R Scott Fusiliers in F and marched billets at LOCRE	
10th	"	do	
11th	"	[In Trenches E KEMMEL]	2 wounded (Rank&File)
12th	"	do	2 "
13th	KEMMEL	Relieved Scott Fusiliers in trenches E KEMMEL	1 "
14th	"	In Trenches E KEMMEL	
15th	"	do	
16th	"	do	(10+) 2 wounded
17th	"	do	(16+)
18th	"	do	(30+) 2 killed 3 wounded
19th	"	do	
20th	LOCRE	Relieved by H.A.C & marched N.Trches at LOCRE	2 "
21st	"	In Trches LOCRE	1 killed 2 wounded
22nd	"	"	2 wounded
23rd	"	"	2 "
24th	"	"	
25th	"	"	

Army Form C. 2118.

WAR DIARY
or
INTELLIGENCE SUMMARY
(Erase heading not required.)

Instructions regarding War Diaries and Intelligence Summaries are contained in F. S. Regs., Part II. and the Staff Manual respectively. Title pages will be prepared in manuscript.

Hour, Date, Place	Summary of Events and Information	Remarks and References to Appendices
26th February '15 — KEMMEL	Relieved 18th Hussars of H.A.2. in trenches E. KEMMEL	1 wounded · Hook r Att.
27th " "	In trenches E. KEMMEL	12 "
28th " "	"	1 killed 2 wounded "

R.W.H. Maj T Althank
Lieut J Symons hit two Bgy / to mark
K 10. W. 35

3/29

7th Inf.Bde.
3rd Div.

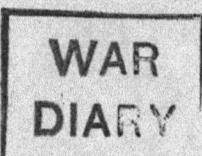

3rd BATTN. THE WORCESTERSHIRE REGIMENT.

M A R C H

1 9 1 5

Army Form C. 2118.

WAR DIARY
or
INTELLIGENCE SUMMARY
(Erase heading not required.)

Instructions regarding War Diaries and Intelligence Summaries are contained in F. S. Regs., Part II. and the Staff Manual respectively. Title pages will be prepared in manuscript.

Hour, Date, Place	Summary of Events and Information	Remarks and References to Appendices
1st March 1915 KEMMEL	In trenches E. KEMMEL	Rank & File 2 wounded.
2nd " " "	do	" 2 "
3rd " " "	do	
4th " " LOCRE	Relieved in trenches by E. Surrey Regt and marched to billets at LOCRE	Rank & F. 1 killed 1 wounded.
5th " " "	In billets at LOCRE	" 2 " 2 "
6th " " "	do	
7th " " "	do	
8th " " "	do	3/29
9th " " "	do	
10th " " "	do	
11th " " "	do	
12th " " KEMMEL (LINDENHOEK)	Marched from LOCRE at 2.30 a.m. & occupied "Assembly Trenches" W. of SPANBROEK MOLEN preparing for an assault on German trenches on SPANBROEK MOLEN. The O.R.'s for the assault were that it was to be carried out by 2 Companies Worcestershire Regt on right & 2 Companies Wilts Regt on left, the remaining two Companies of each Batt'n being detailed one (each) to dig communication trench & captured German trench and one (each) to consolidate & place in state of defence the German trench when captured. The assault was preceded by an artillery bombardment to commence 7 a.m. The assault at 8 a.m. oclock. — During the former we came under constant shrapnel and later came constant bombardment and we — The 13th lay in the assembly trenches all day — they were	Casualties 12 R. Killed Captain R. E. HEWETT Lieut C. B. B. LOSS " C. F. MOORE " W. H. CLARKE " F. B. BURR " T. FREEMAN " E. M. MANSELL-PLEYDELL " M. J. MURPHY " W. B. BARLING Rank & File Killed or died of wounds N. cot men 38 Wounded 99 Missing (Rank & File) 32

WAR DIARY
or
INTELLIGENCE SUMMARY
(Erase heading not required.)

Army Form C. 2118.

Instructions regarding War Diaries and Intelligence Summaries are contained in F. S. Regs., Part II. and the Staff Manual respectively. Title pages will be prepared in manuscript.

Hour, Date, Place	Summary of Events and Information	Remarks and References to Appendices
12ᵗʰ June (cont)	Very wet — & the fog closing off sufficient to the A.B. Coy. Headquarters. Commenced at 2.30 p.m. The arrival troops arrived from 4-10 p.m. Distribution of Battⁿ was 1ˢᵗ Co. (Reinstating) "C" Co. under Cap. GOFF 2ⁿᵈ " " "A" " " HEWETT 3ⁿᵈ " (for digging " "D" " " TRAILL new trench) 4ᵗʰ " (for constructing "B" " " MAITLAND position During the night 11/12 the wire in front or trenches had been wired & new places to [?] were made across the trenches. Proceeding at 11.30 p.m., the leading company (got thus severely tried followed by the second company. They came up the ravine one tumble under heavy rifle mountain Gun fire. Lt. Tebb. [?] — Lt. Tebb. [?] from the first line [?] of the front. Strong casualties recovered but up to 5- P. about up to [?] races with 2ⁿᵈ [?] and 2ⁿᵈ MARTIN [?] Preceded to occupy a position of the first [?] [?] — 2 [?] was now this and gray as the trench & cover in [?] lately overcome. A party had been ordered in [?] resorted the charge which [?] had been attacked & held for the German to first support. After our own artillery commenced dropping a [?] explosive shell	

WAR DIARY
or
INTELLIGENCE SUMMARY
(Erase heading not required.)

Army Form C. 2118.

Instructions regarding War Diaries and Intelligence
Summaries are contained in F. S. Regs., Part II.
and the Staff Manual respectively.   Title pages
will be prepared in manuscript.

Hour, Date, Place	Summary of Events and Information	Remarks and References to Appendices
12ᵗ Mar: (con)	in these buildings killing & wounding a number & scattering the remainder. The party that had gained the trench proceeded at once to block each end & succeeded in holding on for over 3 hours until ordered to withdraw under cover of darkness. They succeeded in bringing away all the wounded from the German trench — Under cover of darkness the Batt was withdrawn & returned to LOCRE. The attack by the West on left had been held up almost immediately on their passing their own wire chiefly by machine gun fire from their left. The casualties were heavy & are shown in column of remarks — All the officers of A Co were killed.	3/29ᵗ
13ᵗ Mar: '15 LOCRE	In billets at LOCRE.	
14ᵗ "	do	
15ᵗ "	do	
16ᵗ KEMMEL	Relieved E. Surrey Regt in trenches E. KEMMEL	
17ᵗ "	In trenches E. KEMMEL	
18ᵗ "	do	Rank file & killed
19ᵗ LACLYTTE	Relieved by NORTHUMBERLAND FUSRS and marched to billets at LACLYTTE	
20ᵗ LOCRE	Marched to billets at LOCRE	

WAR DIARY
or
INTELLIGENCE SUMMARY
(Erase heading not required.)

Army Form C. 2118.

Hour, Date, Place	Summary of Events and Information	Remarks and References to Appendices
21st March '15 LOCRE	de Billet at LOCRE	
22nd " "	do	
23rd " ELLZENWALLE	Relieved GLOUCESTERSHIRE Regt in trenches E. of ELLZENWALLE	Recd 147 1 Recruits
24th " "	In trenches E. of ELLZENWALLE	
25th " "	do	" 4 " "
26th " "	do	
27th " "	do	" 4 " (K.M.S)
28th " "	do	
29th " LACLYTTE	Relieved by R IRISH RIFLES and marched to LACLYTTE - H.Q. A. D. and	" " " 2t wounded
" DICKEBUSCH	A + D Coy LA CLYTTE, B + C Coy DICKEBUSCH	
30th " "	In Billets at LA CLYTTE and DICKEBUSCH	
31st " "	do	

H.L. April 7/15.

R.J.W. Plur T.W. Mark
Com'd'g Worcestershire Regt.

7th Inf.Bde.
3rd Div.

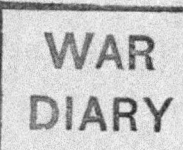

3rd BATTN. THE WORCESTERSHIRE REGIMENT.

A P R I L

1 9 1 5

Army Form C. 2118.

WAR DIARY
or
INTELLIGENCE SUMMARY
(Erase heading not required.)

Instructions regarding War Diaries and Intelligence Summaries are contained in F. S. Regs., Part II. and the Staff Manual respectively. Title pages will be prepared in manuscript.

Hour, Date, Place		Summary of Events and Information	Remarks and References to Appendices
1st April 1915	DICKEBUSH	In billets at DICKEBUSH	2nd Lt. K. L. HALLWARD and one Rank & File wounded –
2nd "	do	do	
3 "	do	do	
4 "	E. DICKEBUSH	Relieved GORDON HIGHRS (1st & 2nd Bns.) and 2nd R. Scots in trenches.	Rank & File 1 wounded
5 "	do	In trenches E. DICKEBUSH	" 1 Killed 1 wounded
6 "	do	do	
7 "	do	do	" 2 wounded
8 "	do	do	" 2 Killed 3 wounded
9 "	LA CLYTTE	Relieved by R. IRISH RIFLES and marched 18 kilos at LA CLYTTE	" 1 Killed
10 "	do	In billets at LA CLYTTE	
11 "	do	do	
12 "	do	do	
13 "	do	do	
14 "	do	do	
15 "	do	do	Rank & File 1 Killed
16 "	E. DICKEBUSH	Relieved R. IRISH RIFLES in trenches E. DICKEBUSH	" 1 wounded
17 "	"	In trenches E. DICKEBUSH	
18 "	"	do	" 1 wounded
19 "	"	do	" 1 Killed 2 wounded
20 "	DICKEBUSH	Relieved by R. IRISH RIFLES in trenches. To billets at DICKEBUSH	" 9 wounded
21 "	"	In billets DICKEBUSH	
22 "	"	do	
23 "	"	do	

Army Form C. 2118.

WAR DIARY
or
INTELLIGENCE SUMMARY

(Erase heading not required.)

Instructions regarding War Diaries and Intelligence Summaries are contained in F. S. Regs., Part II. and the Staff Manual respectively. Title pages will be prepared in manuscript.

Hour, Date, Place	Summary of Events and Information	Remarks and References to Appendices
26th April 1915 DICKEBUSH	In Billets at DICKEBUSH	
25th " 1915 E. DICKEBUSH	Relieved R. IRISH RIFLES in trenches E. DICKEBUSH	R.I.F. 2 killed 2 wounded
26th " "	In trenches E. DICKEBUSH	" 1 " 5 "
27th " "	do	" 1 wounded
28th " "	do	" 1 wounded
29th " "	do	
30th " " DICKEBUSH	Relieved by R. IRISH RIFLES & marched to Billets near DICKEBUSH	K.9 W.1+30

1st May 1915

R.W.W. Murell Lt. Colonel
Comdt. 3/Worcestershire Regt.

7th Inf.Bde.
3rd Div.

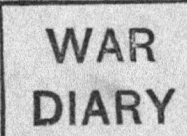

WAR DIARY

3rd BATTN. THE WORCESTERSHIRE REGIMENT.

M A Y

1 9 1 5

WAR DIARY or INTELLIGENCE SUMMARY

Army Form C. 2118.

(Erase heading not required.)

Instructions regarding War Diaries and Intelligence Summaries are contained in F. S. Regs., Part II. and the Staff Manual respectively. Title pages will be prepared in manuscript.

Hour, Date, Place	Summary of Events and Information	Remarks and References to Appendices
1st May 1915 DICKEBUSH	In Billets at DICKEBUSH	R.I.F.L 1 wounded
2nd " "	"	
3rd " "	"	
4th " E. DICKEBUSH	Relieved R.I. RIFLES in trenches, E. of DICKEBUSH	R.I.F.L 2 wounded
5th " "	In trenches E. DICKEBUSH	
6th " "	do	1 wounded
7th " "	do	2/Lt. J.W. SNOWDON & 5th R.I.F. wounded
8th " "	do	2/Lt. H.S. SENIOR wounded 2 R.I.F. killed & 13 wounded
9th " "	do	R.I.F.L 2 wounded
10th " "	do	
11th " "	do	
12th " "	do	R.I.F.L 1 killed
13th " "	do	" 3 wounded
14th " "	do	" 1 "
15th " "	do	
16th " LA CLYTTE	Relieved by R.I. RIFLES & marched to Billets at LA CLYTTE	
17th " "	In Billets at LA CLYTTE	
18th " "	do	
19th " "	do	
20th " E. DICKEBUSH	Relieved R.I. RIFLES in trenches E. of DICKEBUSH	Capt. E.N.L. BROCK killed - 1 R.F. wounded R.I.F. 1 killed, 3 wounded
21st " "	In trenches E. DICKEBUSH	" 2 "
22nd " "	"	
23rd " "	"	L'/Lt. A.R. CHAYTOR wounded - Died 26/5/15
24th " LA CLYTTE & DICKEBUSH	Relieved by R.I. RIFLES (Trenches) & Sig's at LA CLYTTE (2/Lt) DICKEBUSH	R.I.F. 2 wounded (2/Lt)
25th " "	In Billets at LA CLYTTE and DICKEBUSH	
26th " E. VIERSTRAAT	Relieved 2/ SUFFOLK REG'T in trenches E. VIERSTRAAT	
27th " "	In trenches E. VIERSTRAAT	R.I.F. 1 killed, 1 wounded

Army Form C. 2118.

WAR DIARY
or
INTELLIGENCE SUMMARY
(Erase heading not required.)

Hour, Date, Place	Summary of Events and Information	Remarks and References to Appendices
28th May 1915 E. VIERSTRAAT	Dr Reuter E. VIERSTRAAT.	(R't 1 wounded)
29th " "	do.	(R't 4 wounded)
30th " "	do.	(as month)
31st " "	do.	R.2+5. W.2+4
		R.H. Kerr, Lt Col.
		Comdg 3 Worcestershire Regt.
	1st June 1915.	

7th Inf.Bde.
3rd Div.

WAR DIARY

3rd BATTN. THE WORCESTERSHIRE REGIMENT.

J U N E

1 9 1 5

Army Form C. 2118.

WAR DIARY
or
INTELLIGENCE SUMMARY
(Erase heading not required.)

Instructions regarding War Diaries and Intelligence Summaries are contained in F. S. Regs., Part II. and the Staff Manual respectively. Title pages will be prepared in manuscript.

Hour, Date, Place	Summary of Events and Information	Remarks and References to Appendices
1st June. E. Vierstraat.	In trenches E. Vierstraat.	1 R.F. Wounded.
2nd June. E. Vierstraat.	In trenches E. Vierstraat. relieved at night by 5th Bn.	
3rd June. Dickebusch.	Sherwood Foresters and went into huts at Dickebusch. Battalion left Dickebusch and went into billets at Millekappellinen	
4th June. Nr. Vlamertinghe	in "E" huts. Moved to "B" huts just west of Vlamertinghe. Officers went up in evening to look over new trenches near Hooghe	
5th June Nr. Hooghe	Battalion relieved Royal Fusiliers, Royal Horse Guards and Royal Dragoons in trenches near Hooghe	1 R.F. Wounded 4 R.F. Wounded
6th June Nr. Hooghe	In trenches S. of Hooghe	1 R.F. Killed 8 R.F. Wounded.
7th June Nr. Hooghe	" "	1 Killed & 3 Wounded R.F.
8th June Nr. Hooghe	" "	4 R.F. Wounded
9th June Nr. Busse-Boom	Relieved in trenches by 2nd Royal Irish Rifles, and went into Bivouac huts near Busse-Boom just E. of Poperinghe, this was a long march and took relief night very wet, a Bivouac near Busse-Boom	2/Lieut. G. Nash and/Lieut. H.C. Ellis wounded. R.F. 2 Killed 4 wounded.
10th	Do. Do. Do.	
11th	Do. Do. Do.	
12th	Do. Do. Do.	
13th	Do. Do. Do.	
14th	Do. Do. Do.	
15th East of Ypres near Hooghe.	Battalion left Bivouac near Busse-Boom and marched to assembly trenches north west of Hooghe. Sir 7th 2nd Rde. being ordered to support the 9th Inf. Bde. in attack on German line south of Bellewarde Lake. Arrived in trenches 11.45p.m.	

Army Form C. 2118.

WAR DIARY
or
INTELLIGENCE SUMMARY
(Erase heading not required.)

Instructions regarding War Diaries and Intelligence Summaries are contained in F. S. Regs., Part II. and the Staff Manual respectively. Title pages will be prepared in manuscript.

Hour, Date, Place	Summary of Events and Information	Remarks and References to Appendices
June 16th HOOGHE. 4.30. a.m. 7. a.m.	The 9th Inf. Bde. supported by 7th Inf. Bde. ordered to attack the enemy's trenches North of HOOGHE. After heavy bombardment by our artillery 9th Inf. Bde. advanced to the attack and carried the enemy's trenches up to BELLEWARDE LAKE with little loss. Owing to rapid advance of our Infantry and the intensity of our bombardment, our artillery were unable to re-observe and the enemy's third line and part of their second line had to be abandoned owing to our own heavy shellfire on their trenches. The orders to the Battalion were to support and consolidate the positions opened up by the 9th Inf. Bde. The primary object was to support the evacuation of the 9th Inf. Bde. in the captured trenches about Y Wood and to the North of HOOGHE, and help them consolidate. After an examination of the positions had been made, it was decided that no immediate support was necessary. After the answer by the 9th Inf. Bde. the 7th Inf. Bde. had orders to crush their enemy's trenches, and this was done. The H.A.C. at once followed the Battalion and 1st Lincolns and killed them	Killed:– Capt. E.W. Buckler Lt. B. Muir Lt. R.N. Loring. Wounded:– Lieut-Colonel R.F.B. Shave C.B. Capt. J.R.S. Moreland. Capt. S.A. Gore. Lieut. F.S. Pearson. " C.H.D. Banks " E.F. Baldwyn. " L.S. Vicarage " H.H. Millward " G.T. Bennett " L. Walker " W. Walker. Rank and File – Killed. 30 Wounded. 255 Missing 24. Total 309

Royal Fusiliers

WAR DIARY or INTELLIGENCE SUMMARY

Army Form C. 2118.

Hour, Date, Place	Summary of Events and Information	Remarks and References to Appendices
	he could not communicate, but after consistent endeavour was found that no intended support to the H.A.C. which had been asked, was not necessary, as instead reverses in the enemy's trenches occupied by the 1st Batt Balts, new ammunition, more under heavy shell fire, and a good many casualties occurred.	
3.15 p.m.	Our 3.15 p.m. Orders received for the Battalion to push through captured trenches and endeavour to form evening that line somewhere about BELLEWARDE LAKE. Orders were that an Artillery Bombardment on their trenches would begin at 3 p.m. Bombardment was late and did not finish till 3.30 p.m. then "B" Company were under Capt. Maitland supported by "C" Company under Capt. Buchler advanced to attack. The attack was held up by heavy Shell, Rifle and Machine Gun fire, and companies could not advance. Situation was then B & C Companies Coy "Y" Wood. A & D Companies in 9th Bde. Arsenal	

3298

WAR DIARY or INTELLIGENCE SUMMARY

(Erase heading not required.)

Army Form C. 2118.

Instructions regarding War Diaries and Intelligence Summaries are contained in F. S. Regs., Part II. and the Staff Manual respectively. Title pages will be prepared in manuscript.

Hour, Date, Place	Summary of Events and Information	Remarks and References to Appendices
June 17th 7 p.m.	Trenches near WITTEPORT FARM. At 7 p.m. Enemy opened very heavy artillery bombardment on trenches and our line about Y Wood, Railway Wood, and Witteport Farm. Bombardment lasted till 8.15 p.m. and heavy casualties occurred, as many as 90 shells per minute being fired on our position.	
11 p.m.	8th Inf. Bde with 2 coys of the 14th Bde, 4th Div came up at dusk and took up the position won, and at 11 p.m. Battalion was withdrawn to bivouac near VLAMERTINGHE, men very exhausted. The missing men are undoubtedly killed, and were buried during the heavy Bombardment by the enemy.	
" 18th	In bivouac at BUSSEBOOM.	
" 19th	Left bivouac and marched to bivouac ½ mile due South of YPRES. Relieved 7th Northumberland Fusiliers in trenches South of HOOGHE.	1 R+F. Wounded.

WAR DIARY
or
INTELLIGENCE SUMMARY
(Erase heading not required.)

Army Form C. 2118.

Hour, Date, Place	Summary of Events and Information	Remarks and References to Appendices
June 20th	In trenches S. of HOOGE	2/Lieut. G.A. BARFOOT } Killed 2/Lieut. W.W. Meade R+F. 3 Killed 2 Wounded
" 21st	do	1 R+F. Wounded.
" 22nd	do	
" 23rd	do — Relieved by 2/Royal	2 R+F. Killed —
" 24th	Scot. Rifles at 1 a.m. and marched to Gisance ½ mile due S. of YPRES.	
" 25th	In Gisance ½ mile due South of YPRES.	
" 26th	Do.	
" 27th	Do.	
" 28th	Relieved 2/Royal Scot. Rifles in trenches South of HOOGE. Relief completed at 11.45. p.m.	
" 29th	In trenches S. of HOOGE	
" 30th	Do	2/Lieut. F.S.N. Clarke and 1 R.+F. Killed 3 R.+F. Wounded.
	Do	

R.G. Parr. Captain
Comdg. 3 Worcestershire Regt.
July 1st 1915.

7th Inf.Bde.
3rd Div.

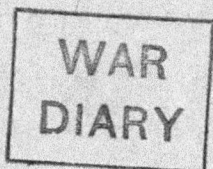

3rd BATTN. THE WORCESTERSHIRE REGIMENT.

J U L Y

1 9 1 5

WAR DIARY
or
INTELLIGENCE SUMMARY
(Erase heading not required.)

Army Form C. 2118.

Hour, Date, Place	Summary of Events and Information	Remarks and References to Appendices
July 1st	Relieved from Trenches S of HOOGHE and marched to Billets near BUSSEBOOM.	R & y 2 Wounded
" 2nd	Relieved by H.A.C. relief Completed 1 A.M. In Bivouac near BUSSEBOOM.	
" 3rd	"	
" 4th	"	
" 5th	"	
" 6th	Relieved H A C in Trenches S of HOOGHE.	
	In Trenches S of HOOGHE Heavy Bombardment of German lines by our Artillery near BELLEWARDE LAKE.	
" 7th	In Trenches S of HOOGHE	
" 8th	Relieved in Trenches by H/S. Lancs Regt Relief Completed 12.15 am. Marched to Bivouac near BUSSEBOOM.	R & y 1 killed
" 9th	In Bivouac near BUSSEBOOM.	
" 10th	"	
" 20th	"	
" 21st	Relieved 1st R. Wark Kents in T. Sector at Sr ELOI Trenches. Temporarily attached to 5th Divn	
" 22	In Trenches	R & y 1 Wounded

WAR DIARY or INTELLIGENCE SUMMARY

(Erase heading not required.)

Army Form C. 2118.

Hour, Date, Place	Summary of Events and Information	Remarks and References to Appendices
July 23rd	In Trenches – Transport in Farm on HALLEBAST. Oudredom Road Heavily Shelled	R & ♃ 4 Wounded
" 24th	In Trenches – German Mine exploded on our Right Front at 9.55 P.M. Trenches heavily shelled	5 Horses killed 9 Wounded R & ♃ 2 killed 10 Wounded
" 25th	In Trenches – Our mine exploded in German lines 40 yards of Trenches destroyed.	
" 26th	In Trenches. German Mine Exploded on our Right Front. Took over Trenches on our left front from 2/R.I.R	R & ♃ 2 Wounded
" 27th	In Trenches.	R & ♃ 4 killed 11 Wounded
" 28th	In Trenches. Relieved by 1/Wilts Regt. Relief Completed by 12 Midnight. Marched into Bivouac 1 mile N of Dickebusch.	R & ♃ 5 killed 6 Wounded
" 29th	In Bivouac 1 mile N of Dickebusch	
" 30th	do "	
" 31st	do "	

7th Inf.Bde.
3rd Div.

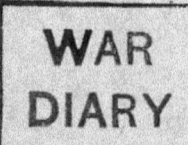

3rd BATTN. THE WORCESTERSHIRE REGIMENT.

A U G U S T

1 9 1 5

WAR DIARY
or
INTELLIGENCE SUMMARY

(Erase heading not required.)

Army Form C. 2118.

Hour, Date, Place	Summary of Events and Information	Remarks and References to Appendices
1st August	In bivouac 1 Mile N of Dickebusch.	
2nd August	In bivouac 1 Mile N of Dickebusch.	
3rd August	In bivouac 1 Mile N of Dickebusch relieved 1st/5th Royal Fusiliers 17th Brigade 6th Division in Trenches near La Brique on night 3/4. Relief completed 12.30am on 4th.	
4th August	In Trenches near La Brique.	
5th "	do	
6th "	do	
7th "	do	
8th "	do	R + F 1 Wounded
9th "	do	R + F 1 Killed 6 Wounded
10th "	do	R + F 1 Killed 3 Wounded
11 "	do	R + F 1 Killed 1 Wounded
12 "	do	(2) Lieut A.M.Eyles wounded
13 "	do	
14 "	do	
15 "	do	
16 "	do	

WAR DIARY
or
INTELLIGENCE SUMMARY
(Erase heading not required.)

Army Form C. 2118.

Hour, Date, Place	Summary of Events and Information	Remarks and References to Appendices
17th August	In Trenches near La Brique.	
18th do	ditto	
19th do	ditto – relieved night 19/20th – Killed 2/Lieut Wilfred James Moon. Wounded Capt C.S. Morice. R & 7 1 Wounded
20th do	by 11 K.S.L.I. 16th Infantry Brigade – relief completed by 12·30 A.M. 20th. marched to Bivouacs near Ouderdom. In Bivouac near Ouderdom.	
21st "	ditto	
22nd "	ditto	
23rd "	ditto	
24th "	7th Infantry Brigade relieved 17th Brigade in Trenches at Hooge on night 24th/25th – Battalion in Reserve in Bivouacs 1 Mile N of Dickebusch.	
25th "	In Reserve 1 Mile N of Dickebusch.	
26th "	ditto	
27th "	ditto relieved 2/Scot Jones in Trenches at Hooge on night of 27th/28th relief completed by 12 midnight.	

Army Form C. 2118

WAR DIARY
or
INTELLIGENCE SUMMARY
(Erase heading not required.)

Date	Hour	Summary of Events and Information	Remarks and references to Appendices
28th August		In Trenches at HOOGE.	
29th "		do.	R+F 2 killed 3 Wounded
30th "		Relieved by 2/S. Lancs. relief completed by 1 A.M. morning 31st August went into Reserve in Ramparts at YPRES.	R+F 1 killed 3 Wounded
30th "		In Reserve Ramparts at Ypres.	

7th Inf.Bde.
3rd Div.

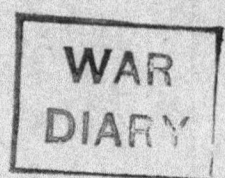

3rd BATTN. THE WORCESTERSHIRE REGIMENT.

S E P T E M B E R

1 9 1 5

Army Form C. 2118.

WAR DIARY
or
INTELLIGENCE SUMMARY.
(Erase heading not required.)

3/Worcestershire Regt.

September 1915

Place	Date	Hour	Summary of Events and Information	Remarks and references to Appendices
	1 Sept		ditto [In Reserve Ramparts at Ypres]	
	2nd	"	ditto	
	3rd	"	Relieved 2/S. Lancs in Trenches at Hooge relief completed by 11 p.m	R&F 1 Wounded
	4th	"	In Trenches at Hooge	R&F 4 wounded
	5th	"	ditto	"
	6th	"	ditto	R&F 2 killed 3 wounded
	7th	"	ditto	R&F 1 killed 5 wounded
	8th	"	ditto	"

WAR DIARY
or
INTELLIGENCE SUMMARY
(Erase heading not required.)

Army Form C. 2118

Instructions regarding War Diaries and Intelligence Summaries are contained in F.S. Regs., Part II. and the Staff Manual respectively. Title Pages will be prepared in manuscript.

Place	Date	Hour	Summary of Events and Information	Remarks and references to Appendices
	9th Sept		In Trenches at HOOGE	Wounded 2/Lt J.N.H. Stone 1 R+F Wounded 5 R+F
	10th "		do	
	11th "		do	Wounded 2/Lieut H.H. McIwadt 3 R+F
	12th "		do Relieved by 4th Gordon Highlanders relief completed by 11 pm	R+F Killed 2 Wounded
	13th "		Marched 15 Billets near Busseboom	
	14th "		In Bivouac Near Busseboom	R+F Wounded
	15th "		ditto	
	16th "		Ditto - Battalion Inspected by General Sir Herbert Plumer K.C.B Commanding 2nd Army	
	17th "		Ditto	
	18th "		Relieved 4th Gordon Highlanders in Trenches at Hooge. relief completed 11 pm.	
	19th "		In Trenches at HOOGE	R+F 2 killed 9 Wounded
	20th "		In Trenches at HOOGE	

WAR DIARY
or
INTELLIGENCE SUMMARY

(Erase heading not required.)

Army Form C. 2118

Place	Date	Hour	Summary of Events and Information	Remarks and references to Appendices
	21st Sept		In Trenches at HOOGE	R & 1 Killed
	22nd "		ditto	R & 1 Killed 2 Wounded
	23rd "		Relieved by 1st Gordon Highlanders relief completed 10.30 p.m marched to Bivouac 1 mile N of Dickebusch.	R & 1 Killed 4 Wounded
	24th "		Marched to Dugouts in 47 Landin Line along the Canal S of Ypres. as Bde Reserve to the 9th Infantry Brigade – Line occupied by 7.30 p.m	Wounded 2/Lieut E.L Bishop. 1 R & 7. Killed
	25th "		In Reserve along Canal Bank S of Ypres, as Bde Reserve to 9th Infantry Brigade during Operation against the German Lines by 5th Corps. Relieved 1st Bn Gordon Highlanders in Trenches at HOOGE. Relief completed by 11.15 p.m.	
	26th "		In Trenches at HOOGE	R & 2 killed 8 Wounded
	27th "		In Trenches at HOOGE. relieved by 1st Bn Northumberland Fusiliers relief completed by 11.15 p.m. Marched to Billets in Busseboom.	R & 3 Killed 7 Wounded

WAR DIARY or INTELLIGENCE SUMMARY

Army Form C. 2118

Place	Date	Hour	Summary of Events and Information	Remarks and references to Appendices
	28th Sept		In Bivouac at Busseboom.	R & F 2 Wounded
	29th "		ditto	
	30th "		Attached 15th Infantry Brigade. Marched at 9 a.m. to Zillebeke. Switch - one Company to Maple Copse in Reserve to 15th Infantry Brigade during Counter Attack on Sunken Road End of Sanctuary Wood.	

Ide Whybugh Capt
2/Worcestershire Regt
30 Sept/15

7th Inf. Bde.
3rd Div.

Battn. transferred
with Bde. to 25th
Div. 18.10.15.

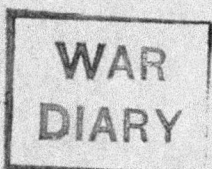

3rd BATTN. THE WORCESTERSHIRE REGIMENT.

O C T O B E R

1 9 1 5

WAR DIARY
or
INTELLIGENCE SUMMARY

(Erase heading not required.)

Army Form C. 2118

Instructions regarding War Diaries and Intelligence Summaries are contained in F.S. Regs., Part II. and the Staff Manual respectively. Title Pages will be prepared in manuscript.

Place	Date	Hour	Summary of Events and Information	Remarks and references to Appendices
	1st October		Bn moved up to Sanctuary Wood and relieved 4th Bn Middlesex Regt — Trench relief completed 10.45 p.m.	Killed 2/Lt C.E.W. Kauntze
	2nd October		In Trenches at Sanctuary Wood	R & 7 1 killed 2 Wounded
	3rd "		ditto	R & 7 1 Wounded
	4th "		ditto	R & 7 9 Wounded
	5th "		ditto	Killed 2/Lt Edward Ernest Vaile R & 7 2 Wounded
	6th "		ditto	
	7th "		ditto	R & 7 2 killed 2 wounded
	8th "		Relieved by 4th Bn Middlesex Regt — Relief completed 11.15 p.m. returned to Busseboom to join 7th Infantry Brigade	Killed 2/Lt Allan Muir Scougal R & 7 2 killed 1 wounded
	9th "		In bivouac at Busseboom	
	10 "		ditto	

R.W. Whybrow Major

WAR DIARY
or
INTELLIGENCE SUMMARY

(Erase heading not required.)

Army Form C. 2118

Place	Date	Hour	Summary of Events and Information	Remarks and references to Appendices
	11th October		In Bivouac near Busseboom.	
	12th "		Relieved 2/5 Lines in Trenches immediately left and centre of Hill 60 - relief completed by 10 p.m.	
	13th "		In Trenches	
	14th "		Relieved by 1st North Stafford Regt - relief completed by 10.15 p.m. marched to Bivouac New Busseboom. (17th Infty Brigade)	Wounded 2/Lieut. K.L. Spiers Y R & F.
	15th "		marched to Bivouac 2 Kilometres h.E. of Abeelle on the Poppringhe - Abeellz Road	
	16th "		In Bivouac Ditto.	
	17th "		In Bivouac Ditto. Battalion inspected by Major General J.A.L. Haldane C.B. Presented The Russian Order of St George (3rd Class) to Serjeant (Acting 3rd Sergt) D.S.O. W. Mansell and made a Farewell address to the Regiment on his leaving the Division	

Whitinghugh Major

Army Form C. 2118

WAR DIARY
or
INTELLIGENCE SUMMARY
(Erase heading not required.)

Instructions regarding War Diaries and Intelligence Summaries are contained in F. S. Regs., Part II. and the Staff Manual respectively. Title Pages will be prepared in manuscript.

Place	Date	Hour	Summary of Events and Information	Remarks and references to Appendices
	17th October	At 5.30 p.m.	Battn marched to Bailleul via. Boesceppe – St Jan's (Continued) Capel to join 25th Division 2nd Corps. arrived Bailleul 9 p.m.	
	18th October	"	In Billets at Bailleul.	
	19 "	"	ditto	
	20 "	"	ditto	
	21 "	"	ditto Battn inspected by Lt General Sir Charles Ferguson K.C.B. M.V.O. D.S.O. Comdg 2nd Army	
	22nd "	"	In Billets at Bailleul.	
	23rd "	"	In Billets at Bailleul. Battalion inspected by Major General Doran Commanding 25th Division.	
	24 "	"	marched at 9 a.m. to the Piggeries relieving 10th K.O.Y.L. Infantry in Brigade Reserve to the left Sector (Ploegsteert Wood).	
	25 "	"	In Brigade Reserve ditto	

Ian Whybrow Major

Army Form C. 2118

WAR DIARY
or
INTELLIGENCE SUMMARY

(Erase heading not required.)

Instructions regarding War Diaries and Intelligence Summaries are contained in F. S. Regs., Part II. and the Staff Manual respectively. Title Pages will be prepared in manuscript.

Place	Date	Hour	Summary of Events and Information	Remarks and references to Appendices
	26th October		Took over trenches from 15th Bn Durham Light Infantry - relieved at Piggeries by 10th Cheshire Regt. relief completed by 11.30 A.M.	Wounded 1 R + F.
	27th October		In Trenches Left Sector Ploegsteert Wood.	
	28" "		Ditto	
	29" "		Ditto	
	30" "		Ditto	
	31st "		Ditto	Wounded 2 R + F.

www.ingramcontent.com/pod-product-compliance
Lightning Source LLC
Chambersburg PA
CBHW081444160426
43193CB00013B/2383